W9-CFB-170

INDIANA LANDSCAPES

Photographs by Randall R. Shedd

INDIANA UNIVERSITY PRESS

Bloomington and Indianapolis

© 1992 by Randall R. Shedd

All rights reserved

No part of this book may be reproduced or utilized in any form or by any means, electronic or mechanical, including photocopying and recording, or by any information storage and retrieval system, without permission in writing from the publisher. The Association of American University Presses' Resolution on Permissions constitutes the only exception to this prohibition.

The paper used in this publication meets the minimum requirements of American National Standard for Information Sciences—Permanence of Paper for Printed Library Materials, ANSI Z39.48-1984.

Manufactured in Hong Kong

Library of Congress Cataloging-in-Publication Data

Shedd, Randall R., date.
   Indiana landscapes / photographs by Randall R. Shedd.
      p.   cm.
   ISBN 0–253–35206–1. — ISBN 0–253–20750–9 (pbk.)
   1. Natural history—Indiana—Pictorial works.   I. Title.
QH105.I6S54   1992
508.772'022'2—dc20   92–8823

2   3   4   5   96   95   94   93   92

Frontis: Woodfern, Martin County.

Editor: Terry Cagle
Book and Jacket Designer: Pamela Albert
Production Coordinator: Harriet Curry
Typeface: Palatino/Weiss
Compositor: J. Jarrett Engineering, Inc.
Printer: Everbest Printing Co., Ltd.

Preface

Some of my fondest childhood memories are of trips to Brown County State Park and the state and national forests that surround my hometown of Bloomington. It seems as though all of my life, as far back as I can remember, the beauty of nature and the changes in the seasons have overwhelmed me. I can remember as a boy sitting in the library at school going through magazines like *National Geographic* and *Arizona Highways*. The photographs were always the most arresting part of any magazine for me. The old adage that "a picture is worth a thousand words" is especially true for someone whose imagination tends to the visual.

Photographs are reference points along an ever changing pathway, and they capture that which constantly slips away. They are my attempts to communicate and register on film that which I am unable to express in words.

During the past ten years, I have spent many days exploring the trails of Indiana's state parks, nature preserves, and state and national forests looking for vistas great and small. My continuous quest was to capture the unaltered, natural, wild, and scenic beauty of Indiana.

After logging thousands of miles wandering Indiana from the Ohio River to the Indiana Dunes in all seasons, do I claim to know it well? My answer can only be, "Scarcely!" My exploration of Indiana has been an eye-opening experience. When I started, I thought I had a pretty good knowledge of Indiana's natural beauty, but the more I explored, the more I found. For each place I have visited, at least a dozen more remain.

The book begins with images from southern Indiana and is organized, albeit somewhat loosely, from south to north. It thus tends to recapitulate the settlement patterns of pioneer times. We begin on the Ohio River and end with the dunes.

I hope my photographs can record nature's most beautiful and transitory moments and serve as landmarks for the future. It is also my hope that those who view the images in this book will be moved to get out and enjoy Indiana's natural areas and help to preserve them.

Randall Shedd

For all who love the out-of-doors, special dawns and twilights, glimpses into the worlds of wild creatures, the slant of light among trees, the glint of sunshine on water, natural beauties in a thousand forms haunt the memory. But the sharpness of these mental pictures usually diminishes; their images become less clear; imperceptibly they fade away. When, in some fortunate split second of time, a camera catches on film the mood, the action, the life, and the beauty of some outstanding moment, it contributes a kind of permanence of its own to a memory. At a glance and after the passage of years, it has the power to evoke the atmosphere, the emotions, the sense of wonder that characterized that instant of the past.

—Edwin Way Teale

Late summer wildflowers at the height of their bloom near Metamora.

Framed by snow-covered trees, this beautiful stone bridge spans the lake at Spring Mill State Park.

*Fall sumac and sassafras along
Highway 62 in Perry County.*

A lone deer stands quietly on a foggy morning at Harmonie State Park.

An old hay roll in southern Perry County near the Ohio River.

Spring wildflowers at Clifty Falls State Park.

The glow of a spectacular sunset at "Big Bend" on the Ohio River at Leavenworth. (Overleaf)

Cypress knees surround an old cypress tree at Twin Swamps Nature Preserve near Honey Lake, Posey County.

The brilliant colors of fall on Wyandotte Lake in Crawford County.

Clifty Creek on its way to the Ohio River at Clifty Falls State Park.

Big Clifty Falls.

Southern Indiana has many knobs that rise abruptly above the farmland valleys. This view, on a foggy winter morning at sunrise, is south of Brownstown on Highway 135.

Cardinal flower at North Fork Waterfowl Refuge, Lake Monroe.

Hemlock falls and huge moss-covered boulders surrounded by a profusion of ferns and wildflowers at Hemlock Cliffs Recreation Area in the Hoosier National Forest.

Sandstone cliffs and rare flora in Yellow Birch Ravine Nature Preserve near Taswell, Crawford County.

In September tickseed sunflowers cover the fields at the North Fork Waterfowl Refuge on Lake Monroe.

Hay rolls dot the landscape in Brown County.

McCormick's Creek wanders its way through fallen autumn leaves at McCormick's Creek State Park.

Jack-in-the-pulpit berries.

Redbuds, poplars, and dogwoods mingle their spring colors in central Indiana's Monroe County. (Overleaf)

The knobs at Jackson State Forest.

33

Morel mushroom.

Mesmore Cliffs in Crawford County.

Purple loosestrife and lotus at Yellowwood Lake in Brown County.

An early autumn snow covers maple leaves at McCormick's Creek State Park.

Winter sunset across the frozen waters of Kickapoo Lake at Shakamak State Park.

Ring-necked ducks at Stillwater Marsh near Lake Monroe.

Winter reflection on Strahl Lake in Brown County State Park.

Old barn at Paragon, Indiana.

The golden colors of autumn cypress mirrored in Starve Hollow Lake. (Overleaf)

Spring hillside at Kelly Hill overlook in Brown County.

Frost patterns as ground cover at Charles C. Deam Wilderness.

Sunrise on the backwaters of the East Fork of the White River.

Snow-covered trees envelop an overlook in Brown County State Park. (Overleaf)

Lower Cataract Falls stand half frozen in early winter—Owen County.

Winter broom sedge, Hoosier National Forest. (Overleaf)

Early spring dogwoods at Brown County State Park.

Wild dame's rocket blooms near Williams Dam in Lawrence County.

Ice cascade along Frog Pond Ridge,
Charles C. Deam Wilderness.

The Narrows Covered Bridge in Turkey Run
State Park, built in 1882. (Overleaf)

Wild iris near the Muscatatuck National Wildlife Refuge in Jennings County.

Autumn color at Shades State Park.

Nature preserve near Shoals, Indiana.

*An old beech tree in Bear Creek Canyon
at Portland Arch Nature Preserve.*

Big Pine Nature Preserve near Shades State Park.

White water lilies, Pigeon River Fish and Wildlife Area, Lagrange County. (Overleaf)

Rocks at Williamsport.

Marsh-marigolds at Pokagon State Park.

One of the many wet marshy woods at Pokagon State Park. (Overleaf)

A foggy mayapple-lined trail at Pokagon State Park.

Fall maple tree, Steuben County.

Sunrise on Eagle Lake, Noble County.
(Overleaf)

Winterberry at Tamarack Swamp Nature Preserve.

A field of blooming lupine at the West Beach area of the Indiana Dunes National Lakeshore. (Overleaf)

A fog-shrouded woods at Kankakee State Fish and Wildlife Area.

*The beautiful willow-lined water of the Elkhart River, Noble County.
(Overleaf)*

Dune grasses at West Beach.

Sand patterns on Mt. Baldy, Indiana Dunes National Lakeshore.

About the Photographs

The photographic images in this book were made with a Pentax 6×7 camera with focal lengths from 45 mm to 400 mm and a Nikon 35-mm camera with focal lengths from 20 mm to 500 mm. The film was Fujichrome and Kodachrome. Exposures were made with both the TTL meters in the cameras and a hand-held Pentax 1° spot meter. Warming filters (81A and 81B) were used in some shaded conditions. A polarizing filter was used occasionally to help reduce glare and increase color saturation.